Before They Were Famous

Mark Twain

Written by Stephen Krensky
Illustrated by Bobbie Houser

A Crabtree Crown Book

Crabtree Publishing
crabtreebooks.com

School-to-Home Support for Caregivers and Teachers

This book is designed to teach and appeal to a student on core subject areas. The student will build upon what they already know about the subject and engage in topics that they do not know but want to learn more about. Here are a few guiding questions to help the reader on his or her comprehension skills. Possible answers appear here in red.

Before Reading:

What do I know about this topic?

- *I know that Mark Twain was the author of the two popular books The Adventures of Tom Sawyer and The Adventures of Huckleberry Finn.*
- *I know that Mark Twain was the pen name for Samuel Clemens.*

What do I want to learn about this topic?

- *I want to learn more about the adventures Samuel had while he was piloting a steamboat on the Mississippi River.*
- *I want to learn more about the time when he was living in Nevada trying to strike it rich mining for silver.*

During Reading:

I'm curious to know...

- *I'm curious to know if anyone else in Samuel's family had a good sense of humor.*
- *I'm curious to know if there are still any steamboats traveling the Mississippi River.*

How is this like something I already know?

- *I know that the Mississippi River is a very important shipping route.*
- *I know that the start of the Civil War changed the lives of many Americans and prompted many to move west.*

After Reading:

What was the author trying to teach me?

- *I think the author was trying to teach me that you must have perseverance and never quit when you have a dream for yourself to achieve great things.*
- *I think the author was trying to teach me that you need to be ready to find other ways to reach your goal when obstacles appear.*

How did the photographs and captions help me understand more?

- *I didn't know that although Mark Twain was a celebrated author he never went to college.*
- *I didn't know that Mark Twain exaggerated some of the facts in his newspaper articles.*

Table of Contents

Piloting a Riverboat

Sam Clemens was working hard — and proud of it. He was twenty years old and an **apprentice** steamboat pilot on the Mississippi River. It would take him a few years to learn his craft, but that time would be well spent. When he was done, Sam would have the best job in the whole world.

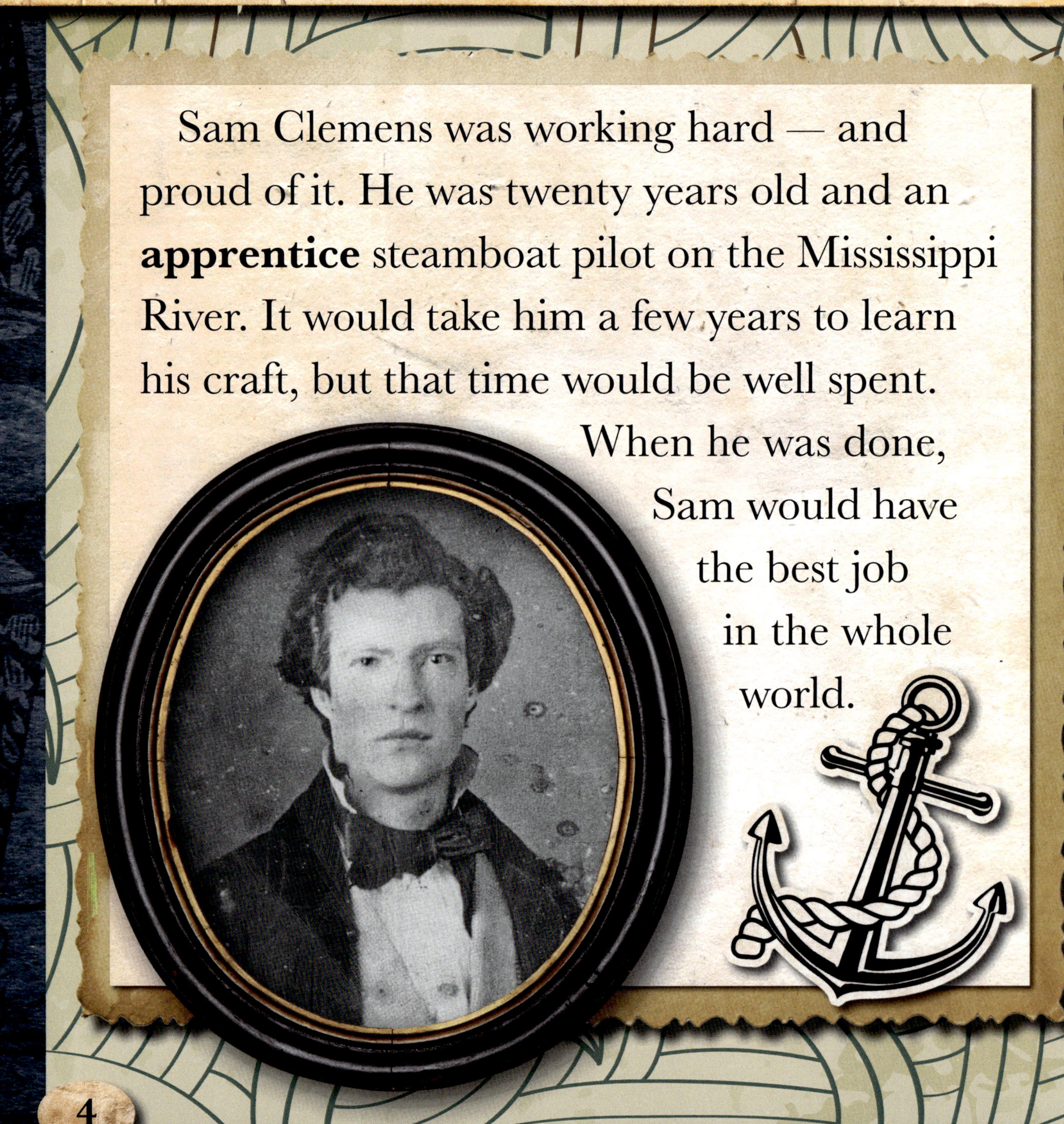

Steamboats along the Mississippi River, 1850s.

Early Facts

Like most young men of his time, Sam Clemens never went to college.

Riverboat pilots had a lot to learn. They had to know the different **currents** that ran over the length of the river, the shape of the shoreline, and the changing depth along the river bottom.

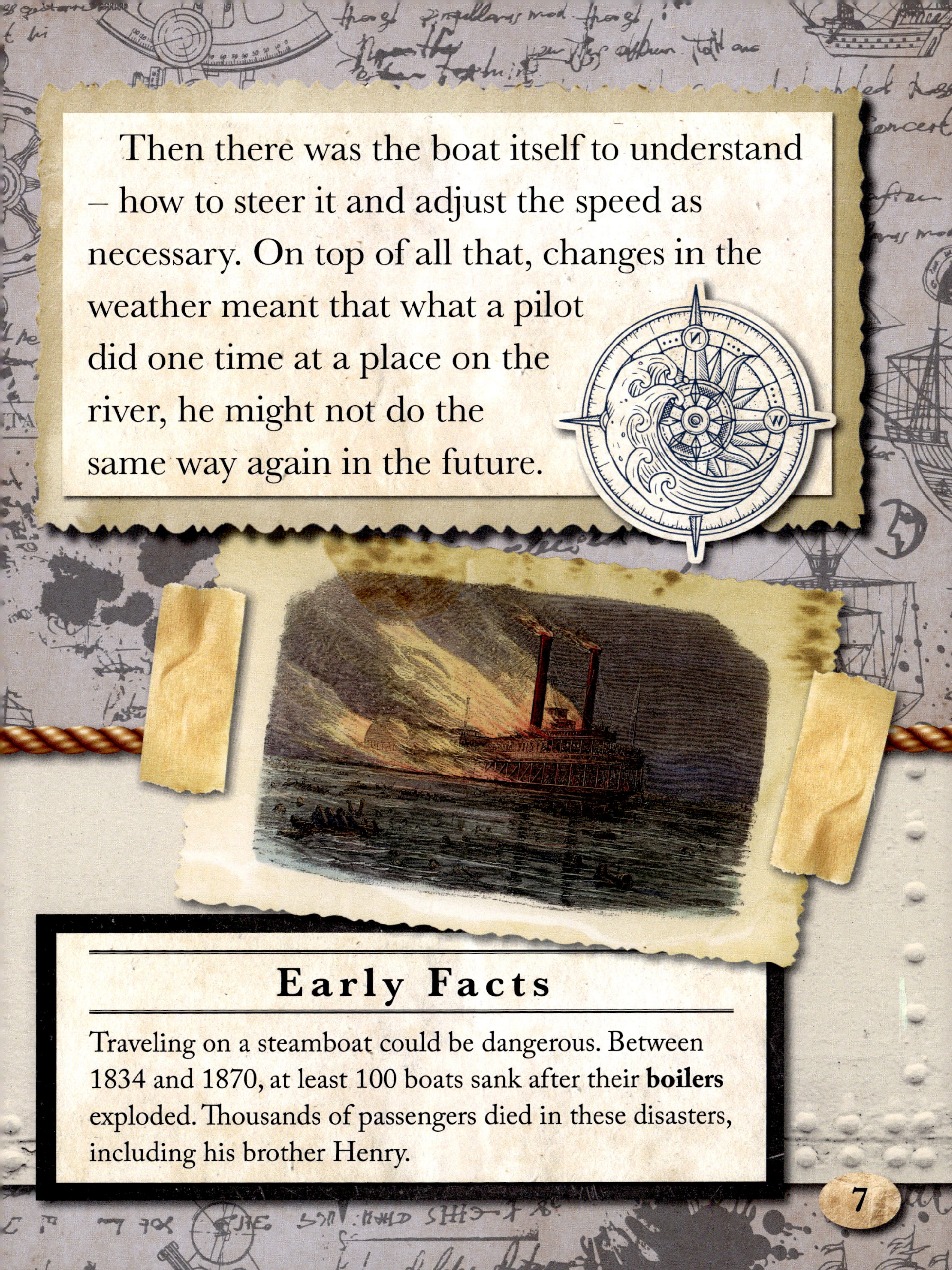

Then there was the boat itself to understand – how to steer it and adjust the speed as necessary. On top of all that, changes in the weather meant that what a pilot did one time at a place on the river, he might not do the same way again in the future.

Early Facts

Traveling on a steamboat could be dangerous. Between 1834 and 1870, at least 100 boats sank after their **boilers** exploded. Thousands of passengers died in these disasters, including his brother Henry.

Growing Up in Hannibal

Sam had always been drawn to life on the Mississippi River. Born in 1835, he had spent his childhood along its western shore in the small town of Hannibal, Missouri. On long summer days, he and his friends spent hours roaming through the woods and fields. One of their favorite pastimes was to pretend they were pirates looking for treasure in the nearby caves.

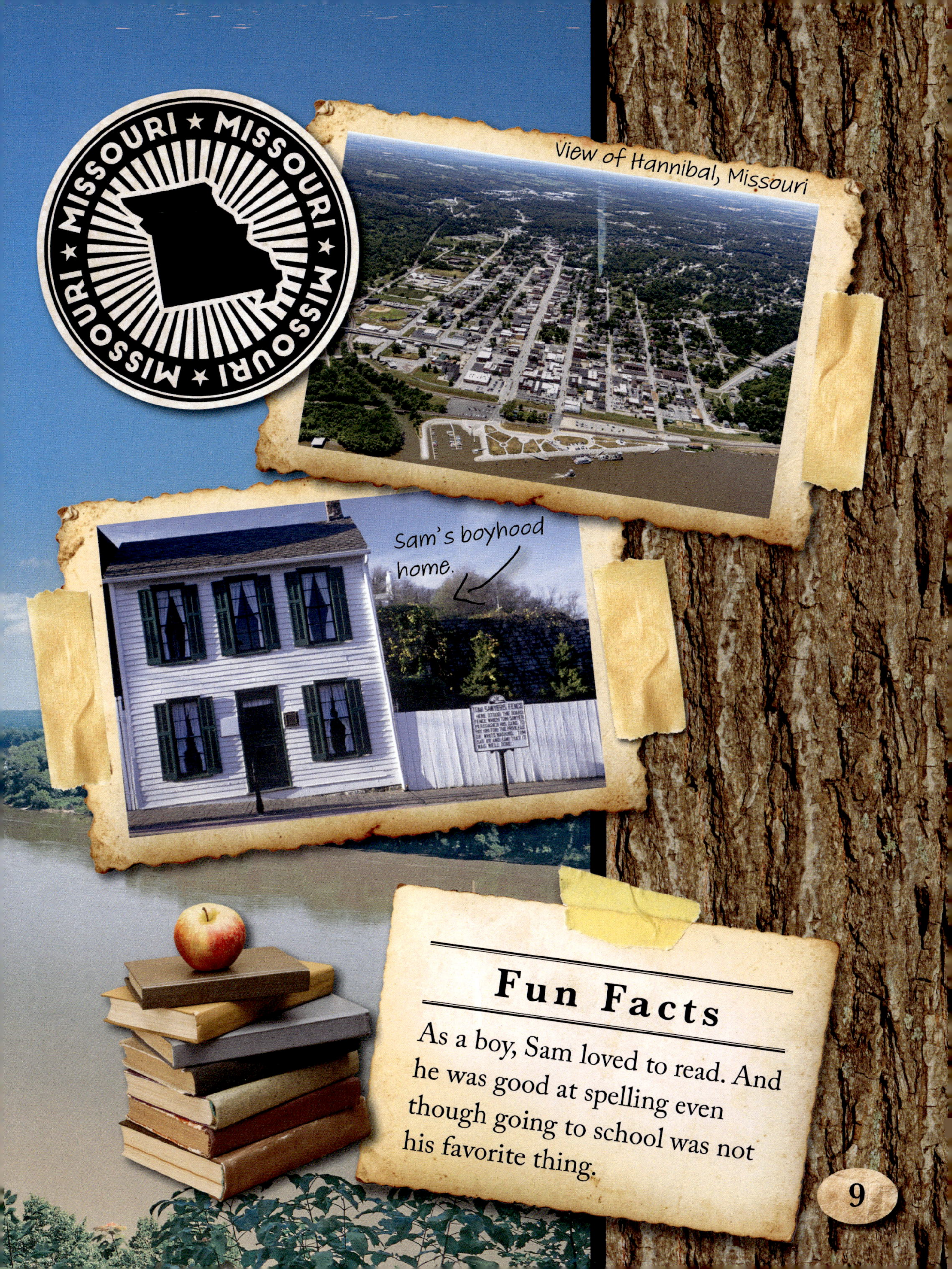

View of Hannibal, Missouri

Sam's boyhood home.

Fun Facts

As a boy, Sam loved to read. And he was good at spelling even though going to school was not his favorite thing.

One winter evening, though, the friends' adventures almost turned deadly. They were skating out onto the frozen Mississippi. But the water that night was not quite frozen enough.

Suddenly, the sound of harsh cracks filled the air. As the ice broke beneath their feet, the boys scampered for shore, barely escaping from the bitterly cold water.

Fun Facts

One time a hypnotist came to Hannibal. Sam pretended to be hypnotized so that he could do crazy things while under a "spell."

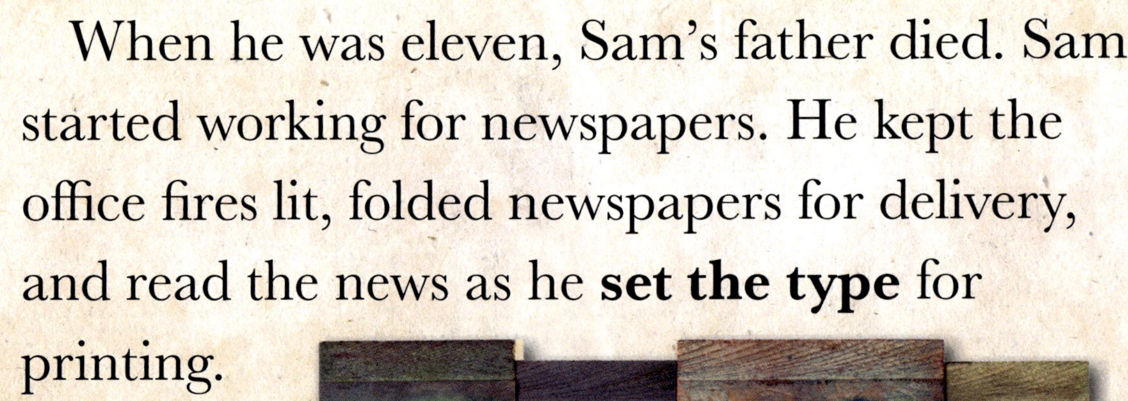

When he was eleven, Sam's father died. Sam started working for newspapers. He kept the office fires lit, folded newspapers for delivery, and read the news as he **set the type** for printing.

For a few years, Sam even wrote news articles. But the pull of piloting a steamboat was too strong to resist.

Fun Facts

One time Sam wrote what he thought was a funny story about someone who lived in town. But that someone did not share Sam's sense of humor and showed up at the newspaper office with a shotgun to discuss the matter.

Home on the River

Steamboats were **majestic** vessels that commanded the landscape of the Mississippi River. Steam powered the large paddle wheels that moved the boats. The first steamboat, the *New Orleans*, was launched in 1811. These boats replaced flatboats which could only be moved by the current. Steamboats could go as fast as five miles an hour (8 kph) upstream, which was considered pretty fast.

Fun Facts

The fastest trip ever taken up the Mississippi between New Orleans and St. Louis took place in 1870. The distance of 1,200 miles (1,931 km) took almost four days.

When Sam received his pilot's license in 1859, there were close to a thousand steamboats traveling up and down the Mississippi. He was very happy as a pilot and believed that he had found his life's work.

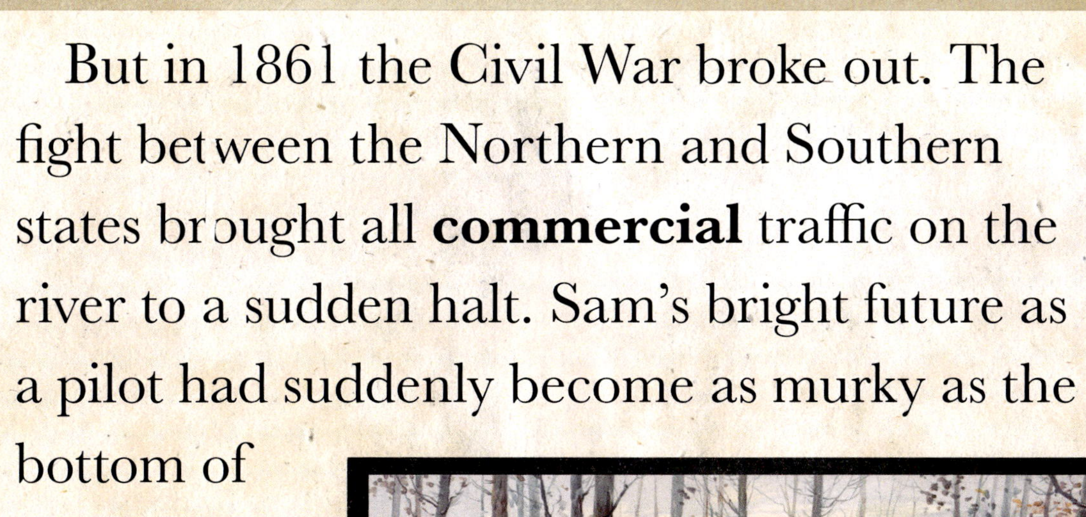

But in 1861 the Civil War broke out. The fight between the Northern and Southern states brought all **commercial** traffic on the river to a sudden halt. Sam's bright future as a pilot had suddenly become as murky as the bottom of the muddy river.

Fun Facts

Two of Sam's favorite things, both on and off a steamboat, were cigars and cats. He was known to smoke more than 22 cigars a day.

Heading West

Faced with the unexpected need to find a new job, Sam decided to head west. He first worked for his brother Orion, who had been made Secretary of the Nevada Territory.

Fun Facts

As Sam traveled west, on really hot days he tried to stay cool by sitting on top of the stagecoach wearing only his underwear.

Orion Clemens

But there really wasn't enough for Sam to do. Meanwhile, silver had been discovered in the mountains of Nevada. Some lucky miners soon started to make their fortunes.

Miners at work in the silver mines of Nevada.

Was this a dream worth pursuing? Sam certainly thought so. Once he began looking, he "expected to find masses of silver lying all about the ground." Sam firmly believed that "in a day or two, or at furthest a week or two," he would find enough silver to make him rich.

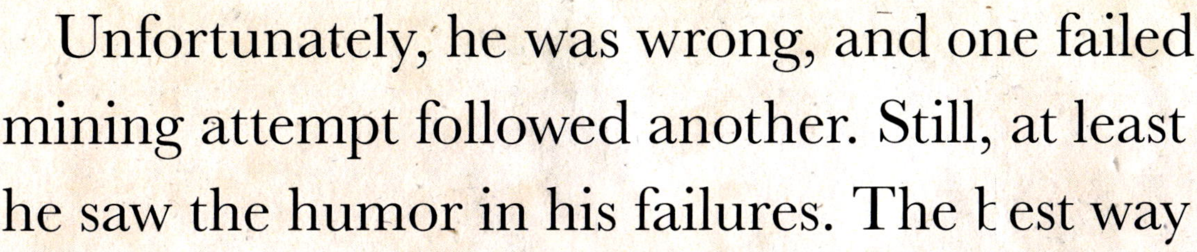

Unfortunately, he was wrong, and one failed mining attempt followed another. Still, at least he saw the humor in his failures. The best way to make a fortune around miners, he realized, was to set yourself up "in the pick and shovel business."

Fun Facts

After silver was discovered in western Nevada in 1859, **prospectors** registered over 17,000 claims during the rush.

Mark Twain Steps Out

So instead of making the news from a lucky strike, Sam decided to start reporting about it. In April 1862, Sam began reporting for a Virginia City newspaper. His job, as he later described it, was "to go all over town and ask all sorts of people all sorts of questions, make notes of the information gained, and write them out for publication."

Fun Facts

Sam was always careful about the words he used. As he said later, "the difference between the right word and the almost right word is the difference between lightning and the lightning bug."

What Sam discovered, though, was that there was a gap between many everyday stories and the drama needed to interest his newspaper readers. So, from time to time, Sam would exaggerate or **embellish** the actual facts to fill in the gaps.

As his success grew, Sam adopted a new **byline** for his writing. He recalled a saying from his piloting days. Riverboats needed enough space underneath them so that they wouldn't scrape the riverbed. But how far was enough? A line dropped into the water with marks on it would show depth. The second mark was a safe distance. The word *twain* also meant *two*. When the safe depth was reached, the crew member called out "mark twain" to the pilot.

A lead line used to measure water depth.

If "mark twain" was the sign of a safe spot on the river, maybe it would be a good sign for an aspiring writer as well. And so, on February 3, 1863, the name Mark Twain first appeared on a byline in place of the familiar Sam Clemens.

Fun Facts

Before settling on Mark Twain, Sam used the name Thomas Jefferson Snodgrass a few times.

Mark Twain turned out to be a pretty popular fellow. To **supplement** his writing, he went on speaking tours for a fee, telling tales of his adventures — both true and not-so-true.

The Mark Twain House
Hartford, Connecticut

HARTFORD
UNITED STATES AMERICA
CONNECTICUT

Fun Facts

Mark Twain wrote his most celebrated book, *The Adventures of Huckleberry Finn*, in Hartford, Connecticut, a long way from the setting of the story along the Mississippi River. It was published in 1884.

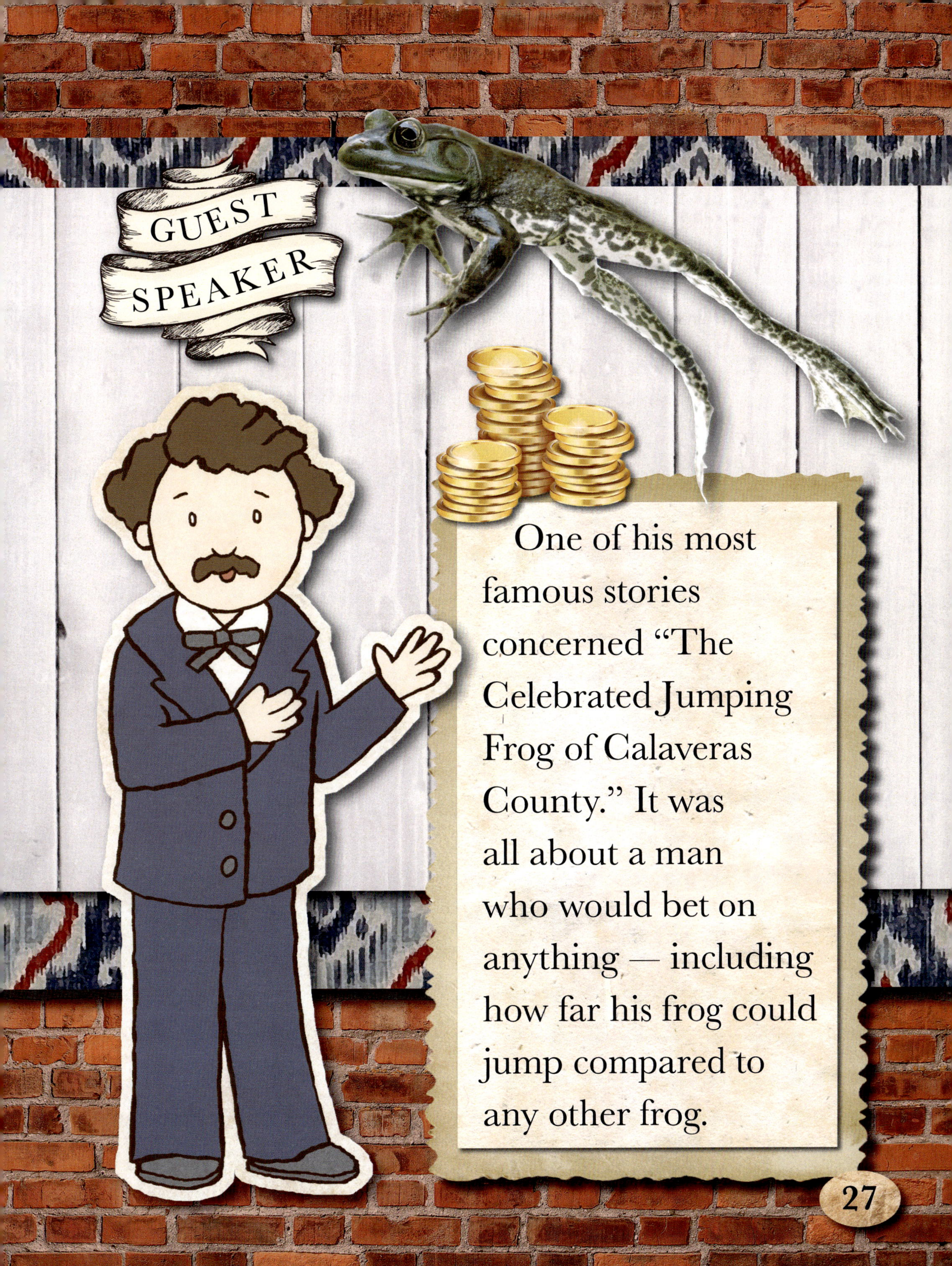

One of his most famous stories concerned "The Celebrated Jumping Frog of Calaveras County." It was all about a man who would bet on anything — including how far his frog could jump compared to any other frog.

Over the next few years, several books by Twain were published about his travels, including *Roughing It* and *The Innocents Abroad*. By the time *The Adventures of Tom Sawyer* came out in 1876, the words "Mark Twain" were more connected to the author than to the measurement.

However, through all his success to come, Mark Twain never lost sight of the challenge he faced every day as a writer. As he wrote in a letter some years later, "To get the right word in the right place is a rare achievement."

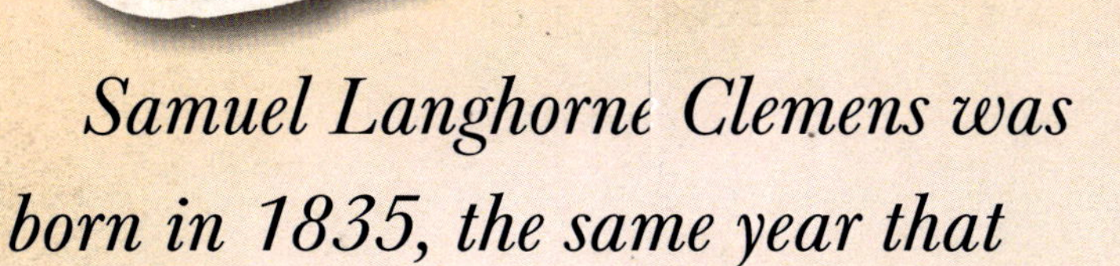

Samuel Langhorne Clemens was born in 1835, the same year that Halley's Comet made one of its periodic visits across the night sky. His childhood in Hannibal, Missouri, provided the background for his two most famous books, The Adventures of Tom Sawyer *(1876) and* The Adventures of Huckleberry Finn *(1884). Although widely known for his* **wry** *sense of humor, Twain endured several tragedies in his personal life, including the deaths of his son Langdon and daughters Susy and Jean.*

Twain lived long enough to look back over a full life, but he knew better than to take it for granted. "The only way to keep your health," he wrote, "is to eat what you don't want, drink what you don't like, and do what you'd druther not."

Mark Twain had always said that he had come in with Halley's Comet and that he would leave when it returned. And, in fact, Twain died in 1910 at the age of seventy-four when Halley's Comet again passed by Earth.

GLOSSARY

apprentice
A person who acts as an assistant while learning a trade

boilers
Tanks that heat water to make steam

byline
The name in a newspaper under the headline that identifies the reporter's name

commercial
An activity relating to business or making money

currents
Water that moves through a larger body of water in one direction

embellish
To make something more attractive or interesting

majestic
Displaying an impressive appearance

prospectors
People who mine an area looking for minerals

set the type
To arrange letters made of metal or wood to print a story on a printing press

supplement
To add to an existing amount of money

wry
Clever use of irony

INDEX

COMPREHENSION QUESTIONS

In what town did Sam Clemens grow up?

When did the name "Mark Twain" first appear in print?

What was the name of the county that was home to the famous jumping frog in Twain's story?

ABOUT THE AUTHOR

Stephen Krensky is the award-winning author of more than 150 fiction and nonfiction books for children. He and his wife Joan live in Lexington, Massachusetts, and he happily spends as much time as possible with his grown children and not-so-grown grandchildren.

Photographs:
t = Top, c = Center, b = Bottom, l = Left, r = Right

Alamy: Colaimages: p. 19 c; North Wind Picture Archives: p. 21 b; Maurice Savage: p. 24 bl; Lebrecht Music & Arts/ColouriserAL: p. 26 br; Historical Views: p. 29 tc; The Protected Art Archive: p. 29 tr; Universal Art Archive: p. 29 br; Granger: p. 4 l, 6 c, 7 c, 14, 15 tr, 15 c, 18, 25 t; Library of Congress: cover bl; Shutterstock: AVA Bitter: cover tl; Vitalii Hulai: cover br; Elena Platova: p. 4 r; D MIND: p. 5 tl; Everett Collection: p. 5 tr, cl, 17 r; Mr Doomits: p. 5 cr; New Africa: p. 5 bl; Fotana: p. 6 b; ekosuwandono: p. 7 tr; Eugene Ga: p. 9 tl; Kent Raney: p. 9 tr; Joseph Sohm: p. 9 c; colors: p. 9 bl; Ola-ola: p. 10 br; Tobias Arhelger: p. 11 tl; jumpingsack: p. 11 tr; HappyPictures: p. 11 bl; marekuliasz: p. 12 t; ledokolua: p. 13 tr, 25 b; chrisdorney: p. 13 l; Black Creator 24: p. 13 r; Triff: p. 15 tl; designtools: p. 16 bl; HiSunnySky: p. 17 l; Vicente Barcelo Varona: p. 17 br; AFstudio87: p. 19 tr; Evikka: p. 19 r; aquariagirl1970: p. 20 l; Serz_72: p. 21 t; Aquir: p. 21 c; Kseniakrop: p. 22; Gchapel: p. 23 tl; New Design Illustrations: p. 23 bl; f11photo: p. 26 tl; JosepPerianes: p. 26 tr; Natalia Hubbert: p. 27 tl; Mirror-Images: p. 27 tr; studiovin: p. 27 br; Volha Nalhachova: p. 28 br; VectorPot: p. 29 tl

Written by: Stephen Krensky
Illustrations by: Bobbie Houser
Designed by: Bobbie Houser
Series Development: James Earley
Proofreader: Kathy Middleton
Educational Consultant: Marie Lemke M.Ed.

Crabtree Publishing

crabtreebooks.com 800-387-7650

Printed in Canada/012024/CP20231127

Published in Canada Crabtree Publishing
616 Welland Ave.
St. Catharines, Ontario
L2M 5V6

Published in the United States Crabtree Publishing
347 Fifth Ave
Suite 1402-145
New York, NY 10016

Library and Archives Canada Cataloguing in Publication
Available at Library and Archives Canada

Library of Congress Cataloging-in-Publication Data
Available at the Library of Congress

Hardcover: 978-1-0398-3889-5
Paperback: 978-1-0398-3974-8
Ebook (pdf): 978-1-0398-4049-2
Epub: 978-1-0398-4121-5